Wintry Mi

For Andrea,
Enjoy reading!
with Love,
Jerrice

For more information, please contact
Jerrice J. Baptiste at ellaninabillie@gmail.com

ISBN# 978-0-9862499-0-7

Table of Contents

Beginning

Sun in morning
Opens eyes to new day
Where heart beats again
Almost in tune with piano

Recalling once again
When fingers reached towards sun   black and white bars

Body now flows with dance
Knows it's a beginning not end of life

Inching closer to sun
Feeling its pull to be one

Absolute oneness
With orb of light and sound.

Before Removed

Christmas tree still stands tall
Beginning of February
Lights silvery balls ballerinas robins
Come alive once more
With violins or woodwinds serenading home

Apparently they miss softness of eyes
No longer paying attention

Before removed one by one
Tree leans towards violins or woodwinds
In effort for visiting family to be seen.

Just Noticing

Thought of fear
Keeps us moving
Closer to being still

Whiteness hovers mind
Conductor in full control takes over
Orchestrating silence

Tolerance of chaos and busyness first
Acceptance arises next with subtlety of her hand
Then noticing beauty of inner silence
During constant movement.

Not Minding, Minding

Over time you start not minding
Lost words   slip of the tongue   memories long gone
Friendships vanishing and appearing like sun.

You really begin hearing vulnerable pitch of baby crying
Holding softness of hand—his or hers
Tone of voice not just words spoken—true friendliness
Toddler rocking from side to side into father's arms

Rocking chair grandfather sat in
Looking out of window
Filled with light of white.

Perfect Pair

Day begins
Hands hold one sock and find its match
Then fold and keep them close together
Perfect pair.

Day ends
Soul touches Soul of mate
Cheek rests on cheek
Lips embrace lips
It's a match
Perfect pair.

Certainty

Footprints left in snow
Follow Story told
Feet placed perfectly in first imprint.

Others before us have traveled
Certainty we're not alone
We go courageously and know
We make it back home.

Company

Dust of white
Sprinkle on earth
When you sit and watch
Mesmerized by love
Heart of Winter lull

Isolation is not even a question
It's company you keep

Beautiful in comparison of any other
Silent and complete.

Cue

Oh what a pity!
When it appears to be
Whatever we can't shake off

Pure white day
Shakes it off

Excesses
Nature undresses

We take our cue.

Plow Again

Four inches plowed
Removes fog in mind—

Sun comes out again
Strings sound differently
Fuller on speakers
Melody reveals

Hidden notes buried
Come on around man and plow again.

God of My Understanding

God of my understanding—
What is my understanding of what you are?

Raincloud melting acres of white Winter.

Bright star
            In billions moving
Silence closer to heart.

Jehovah—Rapha that is sweet prayer
            Gathering circle of sisters.

Lamenting Celtic thought sung.

Poem that is manna on which each
            Word my soul hangs.

Dance that is reverence for this day given
From head shoulders elbows wrists hands
In unison towards new moment.

God of my understanding—
   Rose in vase surrendering pink petals.

Words I say to each pair of eyes—I love you.

                              I love you.

A Waltz

Old
New
Mind waltzes still

In depth sound
Particular movement
Recalling what it does

Brings relief
Freed
    Spirit waltzes this day

Breathe in beauty of sunlight reflected on white.

Among Words

There's life among words
Thriving in blood
Moving through marrow.

There's life beyond despair
Hollowness opens to holiness
Joy mirrors goodness

Goodness in marrow
Goodness flows in veins
Goodness in words
Good
    Nest

Nest is good
Body of words is company
                        Any
                      Many
            Body is company
Love me

Poet
Speak to me
   In your many tongues

Voices
Offer me sweetness

Rich Life—

Needs end
Words enough

There's life among words…

Awaiting

Instead of slippery brown leaves
Feet walk in crunchy slushy whiteness
Knowing body is safest.

Admiring how they fell
Gathered beneath trees
Covered by layers of whiteness.

Snow melts from rooftops branches humbling temple
Sinks beneath soft earth
Awaiting leaves are seen again.

Call And Response
Song of Tinariwen

Foreign male voice sings
Accompanied by flute
Kin in desert echoes his plea—lingering
Pale sun passes through my window.

Foreign male voice sings
Accompanied by flute
Kin in desert echoes his lament—surrendering
Pale sun peaks through my clouds.

In Comparison of Tinariwen

Foreign voices in hot desert
Nomads loving life
Moving through dry lands
In company of each other.

Body of woman alone in cold
Furry head wool neck woven feet
Looking for warmest part of home.

Hearing acappella voices
Drums strings clapping hands

In comparison
All of us living just for today

Body Enjoying Tinariwen
In joy of wherever we land.

Children

Children at play in indoor pool
Living in the Kingdom

Eyes take in
Joy of blue
High pitch screams of laughter
Arms hands legs waving carelessly
Jumping in and out of blue
Forward and backward

Children innocent
Unaware of day
Just aware of play.

Piano Hands Eggs Water

Hands peeling eggs
That's all there is in this moment

Water in round aluminum bowl softens hands and boiled eggs
Hard brown shell cracked on both sides

Hands remove shell in pieces
Delicate white layer of coating follows
So thin, mind must be still to leave no trace
No holes or imprints that fingers were there

Standing in open kitchen
Piano softly audible in background
Where all is abundant and sufficient

Heart takes in
Piano hands eggs water
That's all that's needed in this moment.

In Frozen Lake

In frozen lake, a break
Water appears through

A breath in solitude
A break among noise
Of suffering mind

Juxtaposing the two
Water catches eye
Slows breath
Brief moment of silence inside.

Light Beginning

Violins wash over me
Day is ending
Sound lasting in ears
Even through night.

Recalling words from a friend
Bringing brightness to a world of darkness.

Sound of violins like voice of friend
Remind day is ending but light beginning.

Grace

Hands over head
In serene shower
Signaling for grace
I can get through this day.

Water pours down
Nose inhales under merciful rain
Thankful this rain is there in day's chill

Turning it on
When body needs grace
Water pouring directly on face.

Cocoon

Divine rests quietly in soul
Rebirth with rising sound of strings
Oh how sweet melody
Wakes up being
Life anew
Love to behold
Shifting needless suffering
Joy somehow calls us out of cocoon.

Moon

When moon comes out of you
It's not blue
It's not full

Yet it stands
Not as unique as imagined

It's not wonderland
Nonetheless it's still called poetry.

Winter And All Seasons

In a matter of moments
Thoughts shift
Good bad neutral
Eyes   ears hands
Birdsong lover's poem pencil on table

Why don't we just keep crying?
Endless our joy
Among thoughts dying

Open to it All
Rise my love.

Sharing Morning with Sun

Sun warms face
Feel its rays
Body relaxes with each breath
Consciousness rose on my left
This early morning

Familiar to eyes
Like daily bread in mouth
Generously feeding me and
Peace lily near windowsill

And another plant reaching
Curved long stem leaning
Towards sustaining Life force
Sun warming their skin and mine.

My glowing landscape following its shape
Moving across sky and skylights

Shines on anticipating fingers and mind
Capturing precious moment in words.

Magnificent
Sharing morning with sun.

What Do Poets Do When Sun Comes Through?

What do poets do when sun comes through?

They sculpt beauty that inspires
Words of hope to cope.

Wake up! Sun is coming through
Hope is rising too.

Heat in Winter
Natural elixir
Mind unfolds when sun comes through.

Underneath

Snow covered branches
Bow to piano and strings

Each one catching a bit of sound
Mellow to Crescendo
From moving vehicle's window

Classical sound greeting leafless trees
Reminding day is soon coming
When full love from within returns

Even as whiteness covers
Underneath Joy Blooms.

Sun Salutation

Sweet mother earth
Covered in flakes
She loves this state
Of whiteness
Her Brightness

Politeness seems to be the grace
Of hand holding door
For yogis to walk in
Limber bodies saluting sun always there
It's a deep knowing even when not seen
Its glow
Yogis bow
Breathing in and out
Feet rooted mountains
Arms dive down like swan
Bended head forward
Back tilted as plank
Head goes under
Hands feet spread apart as dog
Breathing in and out
Arms dive up like swan
Feet rooted mountains
Ending praying hands to heart

Sending out inner sun
The joy of being
To others living.

Statement

"The One I Love is Everywhere."
Words spoken by man in
Strange joyful grieving voice

Receiving his wife's love
Who has left her body
But her spirit roams earth.

He feels her love
He sees her beauty up close
In day sky   in snowy shadow of trees

He holds her
In eyes and presence of all
Everywhere.

Pink Blush Roses

Dried petals of pink blush roses
Just as beautiful
In clear vase
Surely alive.

Petals facing all four corners
Of creative room
Where they've opened gently.

Heart of roses sweetened
Livin' in timeless joy of Ms. Vaughn
Strings accompany her angelic voice

Notes of romance
Envelop body of pink blush roses.

Disappearances

The experience is sweet
Eating bread banana egg
Yellow yolk softens on tongue
Gelatinous whiteness disappears

As cloud appears
Covers mid-day sun
Skylight perfectly frames
Moment of comfort
Banana moistens
Roof of mouth delights
Roof of house in expectance.

I Take This Day

I take this day
Where joy is
Here
Not there
Here

Do you see?
Miracle happens here
Not there

Not where mind wanders
Thinks it's better there
Not here

I take this day
And say simply
I accept
Joy
Here.

Singing Bowl

Body sings with bowl
Fullness envelops mind

Reverberating in sacred candle lit room

Easing breath
Out to earth
Holy health.

Breath

Rain drops
Return to breath

Sun shines
Return to breath

Stars beam
Return to breath

Cushioned sacrum
Stay with breath

Right hand
Left foot
Stay with breath

Left hand
Right foot
Stay with breath

Hugging hearts
Blessing with Breath.

Under Sky

Under sky
Breath

Under breath
Sky

Sky breathes.

Under Breath is
Being

Being breath
Sky opens.

Under sky
Being

Being sky
Opens being

Breathing sky
Being opens.

Sky loves being

Being sky
Loves breathing.

Being sky
Eases breathing.

Breathing loves being.
Being opens Sky.

Soft Hearts

Bodies aligned with sunlight
Gentle shuffling of feet
Vertical motion through sunlight
Heel sole toe
Silence within notices silence without.

Slow rocking of bodies
Left to right
       Right to left
Vertical motion through sunlight
Heel sole toe
Breathing in essence of silence.

Bodies at rest
Vertical spines
Cushioned sacrum low to ground
Forming loving circle

Mouths enlighten minds
Soft Hearts.

Minds enlighten mouths
Soft Hearts.

Bowl sings
Echoes in bodies
Facing shrine
Candles forwarding light

Soft Hearts.

Smile

Smile at fear
Buddha knows
Fear needs a big smile

See his face
Where joy within
Knows fear can't win

He smiles and says
"I see and acknowledge you
Like all things
I smile at you too."

Simple

The practice is deceptively simple
Meditate with soft gaze
Shambhala Buddha on cushion
Sitting up like royalty

Yet eyes want to close
Legs fall asleep
Stomach rumbles

Neighbor sitting close slouches
Your own body follows.

Presence of mind is noticing all of these
Things considered annoying

Presence is hearing
Throat clearing   mouth swallowing
Humming of woods this night

Presence is acceptance of slouching,
Rumbling stomach   woods   night sky
And still feel like royalty.

Touch And Go

Humming of heater
Touch and go
Return to breath

Moving toes in socks
Touch and go
Return to breath

Noticing branch heavily weighted by snow
Touch and go
Return to breath

One candle lit   the other one not
Touch and go
Return to breath

Yawning of neighbor's mouth
Touch and go
Return to breath

Next moment in mind
Touch and go
Return to breath

Future life with mate
Touch and go
Return to breath

Past suffering in mind
Touch and go
Return to breath

Future delight in mind
Touch and go
Return to breath

Oh Dear! Impermanence
Touch and go
Return to breath.

What Does One Do When Laughing
In A Meditation Becomes Unavoidable?

Amusing thoughts come
Chuckles begin in throat
Stomach trembles wanting to hold it in.

Sometimes just that we're all sitting doing nothing
Can get it going.

We take it so seriously
Laughing at it All is great relief.

Even if it's below zero
Run out and laugh!

We Find It

Somewhere there's life
We want to find it

In open sky
One beetle crawling not minding the cold—let it live

Brief space between notes of piano
Importance given to words written
Lover's eyes do not dim 'till mine

We find it
We find it.

Deer

Deer in snow
Curved head
Enjoying what is left
Found in land
Of the living

Hope arising
In seeing through woods
Beautifully angled body
Elegance in motion.

Harp On Skin

Fingers softly pluck harp
Fingers of my love gently tap along

Harp caresses mind
Fingers of my love follow along mine
Softness of hand mimicking softness of sound

Harp surrounding ears
Becoming One with skin.

Walking Meditation

Heel Sole Toe
Heal Sole Toe
Heal Soul Toe
Heal Soul Grow.

How Do You?

How do you move?

Fast
Slow
Free

How do you feel?

He
She
Me
We
Free

How do you speak?

Fast
Slow
      Free

How do you write?

Short
Long
Song
Poem
      Freedom

How do you dream?

Small
Big
In between

      My Queen
My king
      My Kin.

Trash

On ice like life
It's a balancing act

Frozen you become if you let it
Won't even throw away trash

Walking on icy pavement
Two full trash bags in hands
Garbage cans seem further away than before

Yet we make it
At end of driveway

It would be easier to drive to it
You would think—

But car skidding on ice
Smelling like trash
Not pleasant

Walking on ice is challenging
But a better balancing act.

Not Quite

We certainly know Spring will come
Floral songs will be sung   hyacinth offering delicious scent
Hummingbirds exploring around gardens

It will all seem new again
Yet it all begins already
Not quite dormant

Bodies are kind of like that
Seem hibernating

Growth can be seen even through darkness

Soul deepens.

The Truth About Wipers

Two wipers stick out
Only things seen
Car buried under snow

When they wipe away whatever comes
Snow sleet rain hail
You see clearly

Death is not here
Wipers clear way for livin'.

Hercules

Even as I write
Hercules drives his snowplow truck
Clearing our two driveways
 I've decided this name fits him best.

Achilles is his real name.

Digging deep each year
Pushing pedals down
Ankles must be strong.

Trust

Water drips from suspended bridge
Its body holds vehicles people
Weather that eventually melts

Yet we trust bridges won't collapse
We take many chances

Even when storms hit us
Amazingly we're deeply rooted.

Asparagus

After three o'clock in afternoon
Eating asparagus
Keeps awake

Bladder fills up
Can't place attention
Anywhere else on body

Not a good idea
If word diuretic won't leave mind
While listening to ice melt at night
Drop by drop from rooftop.

Stimulating Day

Scent of coffee
Bombards air

Living room welcomes it all
Japanese style oak coffee table   red mugs   ornate oriental rug
Happily married couple and strong scent of coffee brewed.

Nose of wife and mind detest coffee
Husband loves fresh taste on tongue

Beyond a decade unfolds and holds
Being snowed in with inescapable smell of stimulant   snoring
Whining about curtains needing to be hung   needing help
with directions

Sold in local store
Grounded as far back as Ethiopia
Joy and warmth of black flowing in his body.

Looking out together windstorm of white flakes blowing
It's speechless beauty.

Sake of love we savor it all.

Summer Reclines

Two summer lawn chairs supported joyful friends
They brought meal to welcome us in first sunny home
Set it on bare table
Brown rice broccoli wings drumsticks smothered in soy
sauce.

On our deck now   lawn chairs and round table smothered by
snow
Underneath thick layers of white
Taste of summer still reclines even when bodies are gone.

Enlightened Society

Icicles hang in long strand
Imagining air catching water as it leaps
Giving it solid shapely body
Close family of different sizes
Thin large small wide short long

Each one sparkles
Eyes are drawn to personalities
Shining rough diamonds
Out of window of home   perimeter of temple.

Hands come together to clear out temple
Thin large small wide short long
Shaking dust out of cushions for resting sacrum
Wiping down shrine   sweeping oak floor

Ears drawn to colorful personalities in conversations
Family of friendly strangers gathered
Temple shines out of our kindness
Enlightened Society Day.

Glow of love within reflected without
Diamonds in the rough shining   overcoming fear each second
With each shared word and gaze taking a leap in life
Timid female voice describes "Overcoming fear is like jumping
off a cliff."

Watching family of icicles suspended in air
Beautiful courageous leaps
Enlightened society gathers around this day.

Cycle

Late afternoon sun shines on icicles
Deeply attached to roof above balcony
Pointed towards earth

Sharp edges begin to lose shape
Small drops

One
　By
　　One

Will bring end
Whether they want to welcome light

Nature brightens   loosens even when we resist.
Softness   Letting go essential part of cycle of rebirth.

Given

For now trees endure coldness
Nothing can be done
It's about accepting pureness
What nature has given.

This day and others
Out of our control

We stand strong
Roots bifurcating
Winds hitting branches

Year after year
Seasons changing
Branches bend break grow

Love
Given taken deepens.

Ocean of Winter

Icicles seem to drip in synchronization with tune of piano
Beyond fire place   Looking out of living room
perimeter of roof

Seeing these small rain drops
What fun it would be standing underneath with umbrella
Or stick out tongue and swallow each

One
   by
     One

Innocent play
Childhood imagination stirred up

Jumping in puddles   muddy boots   soaked tongue

Even catching each
Filling up buckets
Ocean of Winter.

Dream A Little Dream

I won't write another sad poem about Winter.

Malaise   somber moods   shorter afternoons   wider yawns
Unbearable likeness of sweaters   coats   hats   gloves   bearded
men.

From child's perspective it's beauty—
Daydreaming and living

Skiing on slopes, sledding down hills
Heading straight for walls   pine trees
Not caring about ends or broken limbs

They enjoy it.

Day of Warmth

Inhaling incense inside glowing temple
Temple of body
Soothed by sweetness
A moment—absence of torment.

Calming experience enhanced by
Sound of drops becoming streams
Babbling brook lets us know
Gentle warmth of approaching season.

Jerrice J. Baptiste
Poet, Educator, Founder
& Facilitator of Authentic Poetry

Jerrice has enjoyed writing poetry since childhood. Her poetry in English, French and Haitian Creole has been selected and used for numerous educational, therapeutic and cultural purposes. A resident of the Hudson Valley, NY, Jerrice is the producer and host of Women of Note on WKZE, 98.1 FM in Red Hook, NY. She is the author of *Tu Es Ma Belle – You Are My Beautiful.*